Joseph Rosa

# XEFIROTARCH

design series 4

## SFMOMA design series

*Xefirotarch* is the fourth in a series of exhibitions and accompanying publications intended to highlight the work of architects, industrial designers, and graphic designers at the forefront of their respective disciplines. This volume is published on the occasion of the exhibition *Xefirotarch / design series 4*, organized by Joseph Rosa, guest curator, and Ruth Keffer, acting department head, architecture and design, and on view March 31 through September 17, 2006, at the San Francisco Museum of Modern Art.

Previous books in the series:
**ROY / design series 1**
**Yves Béhar fuseproject / design series 2**
**2x4 / design series 3**

Exhibition venues:
San Francisco Museum of Modern Art
MAK—Austrian Museum of Applied Arts / Contemporary Art, Vienna
Architectural Association, London
The Art Institute of Chicago

*Xefirotarch / design series 4* is generously supported by Christine and Michael Murray, Nancy and Steven H. Oliver, the LEF Foundation, and an anonymous donor.

Director of Publications: Chad Coerver
Managing Editor: Karen A. Levine
Design: Jennifer Sonderby with Terril Neely
Publications Coordinator: Lindsey Westbrook
Printed and bound in Canada by Hemlock Printers

Front cover: Busan Concert Hall, 2003–4, Busan, South Korea, lobby interior
Inside cover: Cell Concept, 2005–6, renderings of display system
Overleaf: Cell Concept, 2005–6, wire diagram of display system

Unless otherwise noted, all images are provided courtesy Xefirotarch. *Emotional Rescue* photos by Joshua White; *Sur* photos by Robert Mezquiti and Larry Link.

Library of Congress Cataloging-in-Publication Data
Rosa, Joseph.
   Xefirotarch / Joseph Rosa.
     p. cm. — (Design series ; 4)
   Catalog of an exhibition at the San Francisco Museum of Modern Art Mar. 31–Sept. 17, 2006, and at MAK, Vienna, the Architectural Association, London, and the Art Institute of Chicago in 2007–8.
   Includes bibliographical references.
   ISBN 0-918471-79-6
   1. Xefirotarch (Studio)—Exhibitions. 2. Díaz Alonso, Hernán—Exhibitions. 3. Architecture, Modern—21st century—Designs and plans—Exhibitions. 4. Design—History—21st century—Exhibitions. I. Díaz Alonso, Hernán. II. Xefirotarch (Studio). III. San Francisco Museum of Modern Art. IV. Title. V. Series: SFMOMA design series ; 4.
NA737.X44A4 2006
720.92'2—dc22

2006000399

# CONTENTS

PROJECTS

EMOTIONAL RESCUE       BONDIS BUS SHELTERS       JUMPING JACK FLASH WATCH

LEXINGTON METROPOLITAN PLAZA       LANDMARK TOWER / U2 STUDIO

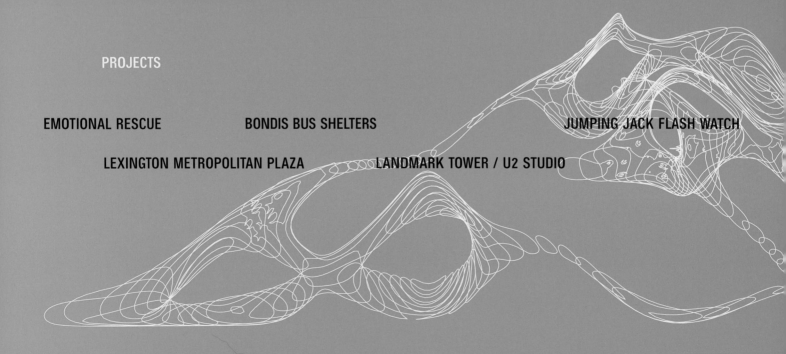

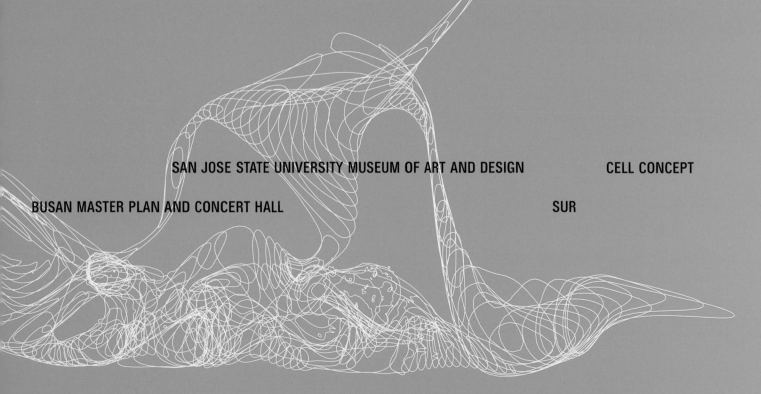

SAN JOSE STATE UNIVERSITY MUSEUM OF ART AND DESIGN          CELL CONCEPT

BUSAN MASTER PLAN AND CONCERT HALL                                    SUR

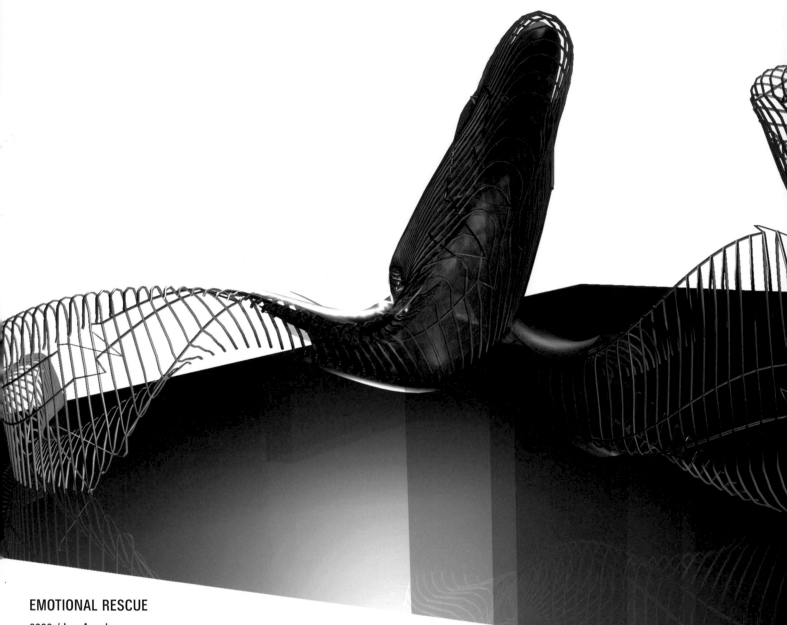

# EMOTIONAL RESCUE

### 2002 / Los Angeles

Xefirotarch installed *Emotional Rescue* in the gallery at the Southern California Institute of Architecture in 2002. A scaffolding of curved copper pipes, partially sheathed in translucent plastic, snaked through the narrow room. The podlike enclosures formed by the sheathing contained bouquets of fresh roses that were left to bloom and decay. The overtly sculptural qualities of the design, titled after a Rolling Stones song, orchestrated a deliberately disorienting sensory experience within the space.

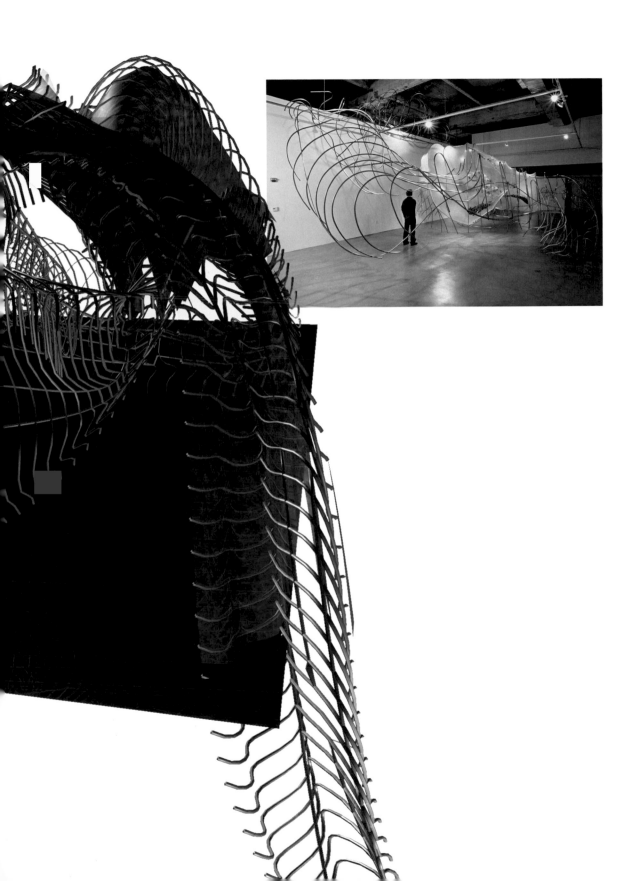

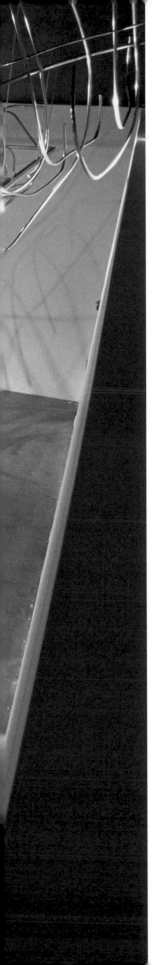

From left: *Emotional Rescue*, installation views; Lexington Metropolitan Plaza, rendering of ground-level enclosures

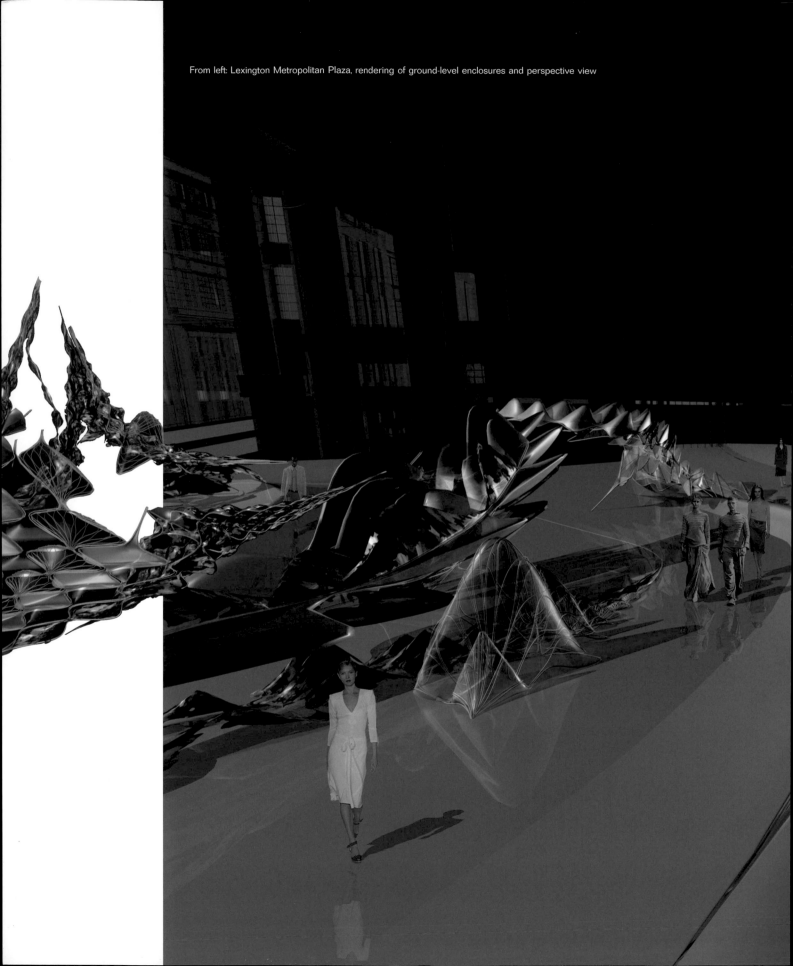

From left: Lexington Metropolitan Plaza, rendering of ground-level enclosures and perspective view

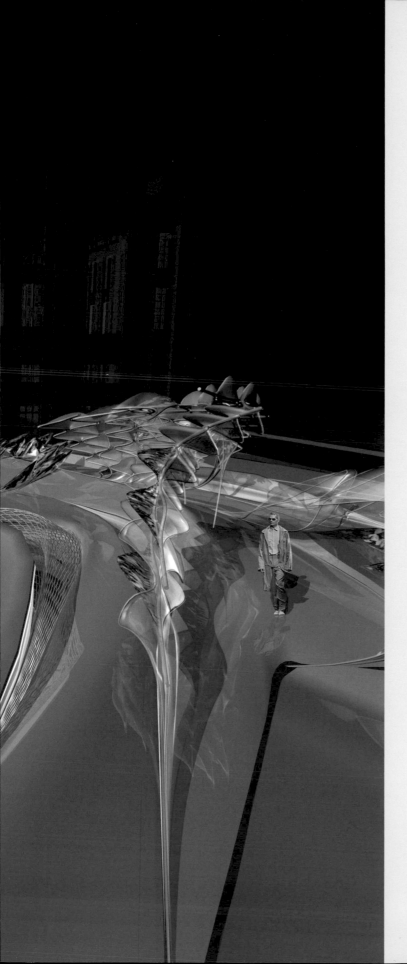

## LEXINGTON METROPOLITAN PLAZA
### 2001–4 / Lexington, Kentucky

This project, the winner of a competition to design a public square for downtown Lexington, was the first in a series of topographic explorations and studies in surface manipulation undertaken by the studio. Xefirotarch imagines the plaza as a long, rippled piece of fabric aligned with county and district court buildings on a busy pedestrian block. The contours of its wavy surface incorporate and reconfigure neighborhood foot traffic, creating a new space for public interaction as people move to and from work and other destinations.

Hidden within the central confines of the plaza are opportunities for retreat, meditation, and refreshment: seating areas, reflecting pools, and even vending machines accommodated by the eccentric topography of the undulating surface. The ripples are actually three-dimensional extensions sprouting upward from the two-dimensional domain of the pedestrian footpath at ground level. The studio exploits this verticality to create extra-architectural spaces where rest and recreation are interwoven with work and movement, effectively morphing the pedestrian plaza into a fully functional park.

Lexington Plaza evolved dramatically as Xefirotarch developed other designs in the wake of the competition. In the 2002 Bondis Bus Shelters project, for example, a single surface folds over itself to create a series of enclosed volumes; the installation *Emotional Rescue*, completed the same year, elongates and extends the volumes while also incorporating flowers as evocative decorative elements. All of these components became part of successive iterations of the Lexington Plaza design. The current plan merges the two- and three-dimensional elements of the plaza and the park, resulting in a complex urban environment where multiple architectural programs intersect and multiple personal and public narratives unfold.

Though Xefirotarch's design won the competition in 2001, city officials chose not to award the commission to the studio, and the project remains unrealized.

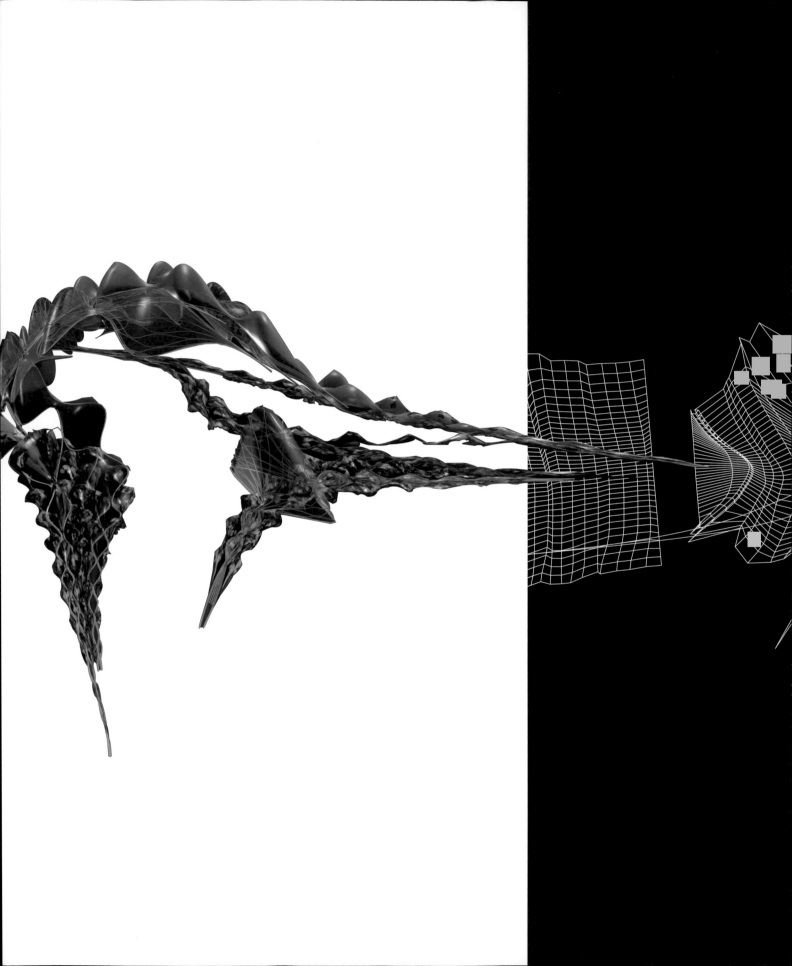

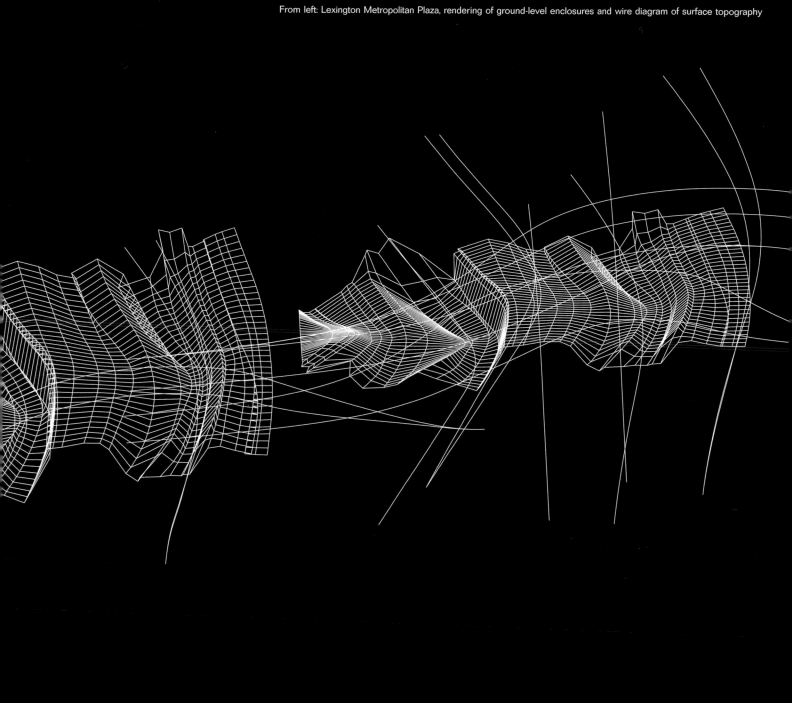

From left: Lexington Metropolitan Plaza, rendering of ground-level enclosures and wire diagram of surface topography

# BONDIS BUS SHELTERS

**2002 / New York**

This project was Xefirotarch's entry in a competition sponsored by the online design magazine *Core77*. The concept for a series of fifteen bus stops in Manhattan evolved from computer-based surface and topographic studies related to Lexington Metropolitan Plaza. The structure of the first shelter is formed by a single surface that folds over itself, and each subsequent design reiterates the same formal principle. One would only be able to view the entire sequence of shelters by riding the bus route from start to finish.

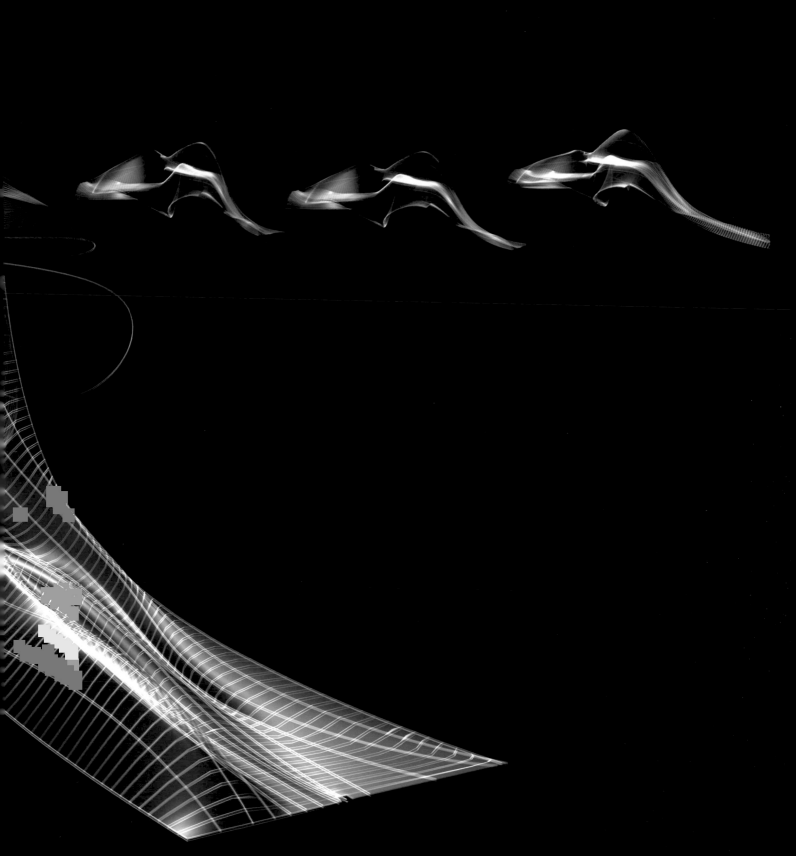

## LANDMARK TOWER / U2 STUDIO

### 2002 / Dublin, Ireland

This multistory, glass-enclosed tower is an early example of Xefirotarch's assertion that architecture can be modeled on biology. Shaped like a dragon, the proposed structure seems to inhabit its site like an animal crouched at the ready. Commercial and residential spaces—lofts, shops, offices, restaurants, and a recording studio—intermingle on the upper levels, and a series of pedestrian lobbies creates a dynamic continuum with the urban surroundings.

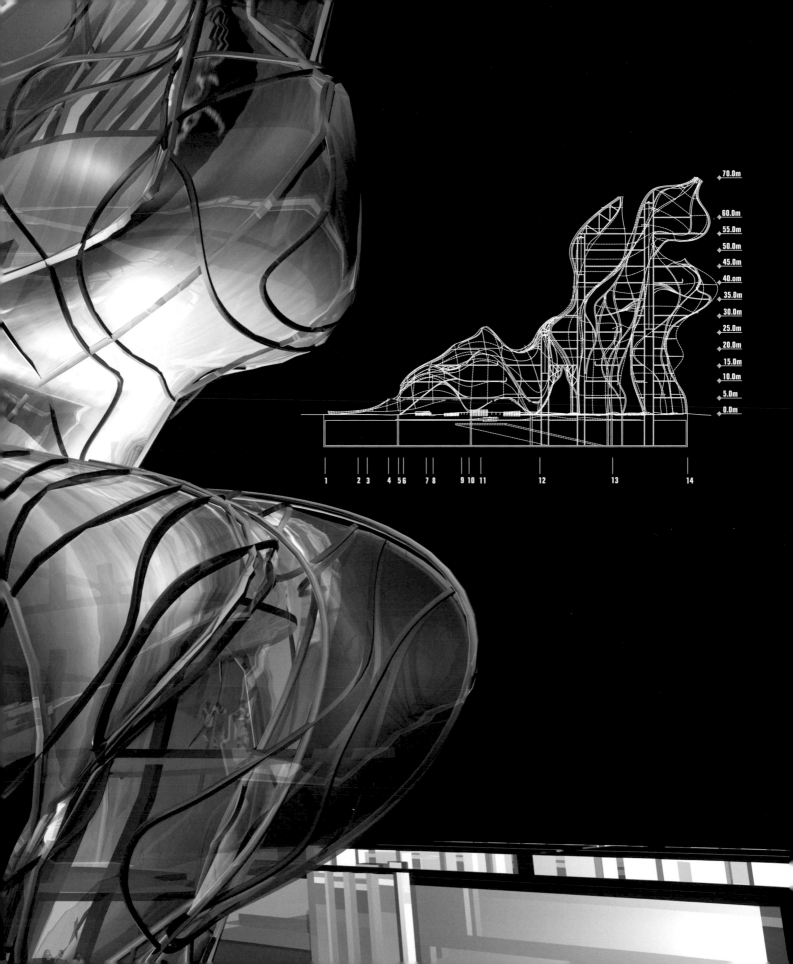

## JUMPING JACK FLASH WATCH

### 2004–

In 2004 *Core77* and Timex invited designers to create concept watches for the year 2154. Xefirotarch's competition entry reinvented a very old technology: the hourglass. In the metronome arm of this grotesquely shaped timepiece, tiny bubbles stand in for grains of sand, shifting back and forth between the lobes in a regular movement. The time of day appears as a luminous projection on the arm's interior face. The mechanics of the watch continue to evolve as Xefirotarch reworks the design for potential commercial clients.

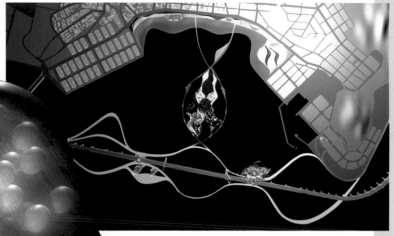

## BUSAN MASTER PLAN AND CONCERT HALL

### 2003–4 / Busan, South Korea

In 2003 Xefirotarch proposed a redesign of Busan's Gwangalli Waterfront, a bustling commercial and recreational area that encompasses Gwangalli Beach and the Gwangan Grand Bridge. The studio's master plan includes ferry and cruise-ship terminals; a meandering pedestrian concourse with parks and a viewing tower; a redeveloped beachscape with volleyball, tennis, and soccer facilities; a hotel and convention center; and a multi-purpose concert hall. The design for this network of varying programs is inspired by the beach environment itself; it is imagined as a web of intersecting eddies that pool together at moments of peak confluence to form islands of activity.

At the center of this web, forming its own small island between the bridge and the beach, is the most prominent feature of the master plan: the concert hall. Conceived as the "jewel" in a family of related forms, the facility accommodates 12,000 people and offers 360-degree views of the surrounding waterfront. Like the amphibious creature it resembles, the hall is an intermediary between city and sea, serving as a porous hub for the ebb and flow of pedestrians, commuters, conventioneers, vacationers, and day-trippers. This "field" of circulation vectors is articulated as a collection of amorphous cells rather than as a simple geometric volume. The dynamically undulating, intersecting, and overlapping spaces—which contain restaurants, shops, indoor and outdoor terraces, lobbies, and offices—all converge on the massive, bulbous forms that house the theater and auditorium. The overall space is disorienting but spectacular, a theatrical experience in its own right.

The Busan project has spawned a number of other Xefirotarch experiments. The 2005 installation *Sur*, for example, offered an opportunity to test—on a smaller, sculptural scale—the idea of architecture based on cell proliferation. Later projects have applied the concept of cellular mutation to various iterations of biomorphic design. The 2005 Cell Concept, for instance, uses a morphing honeycomb structure as the basis for a customizable wall display system.

From left: Busan Concert Hall, longitudinal perspective, lobby interior, perspective view, and oblique perspective

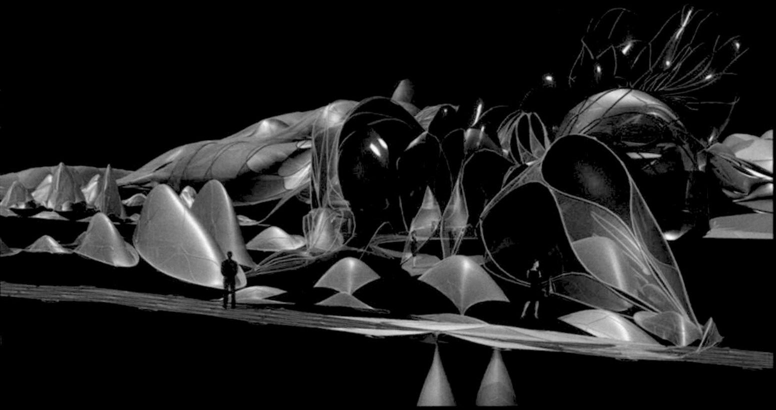

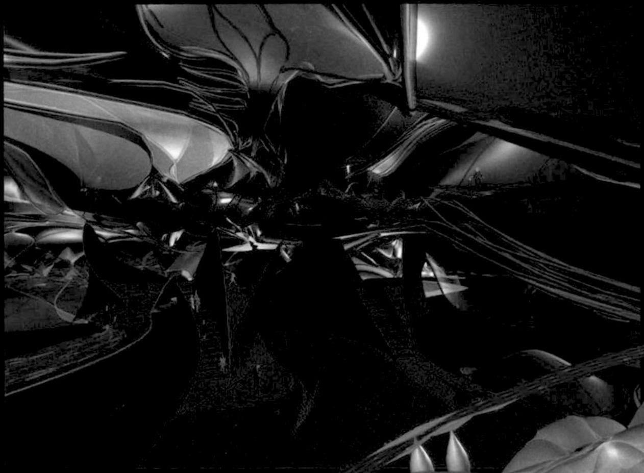

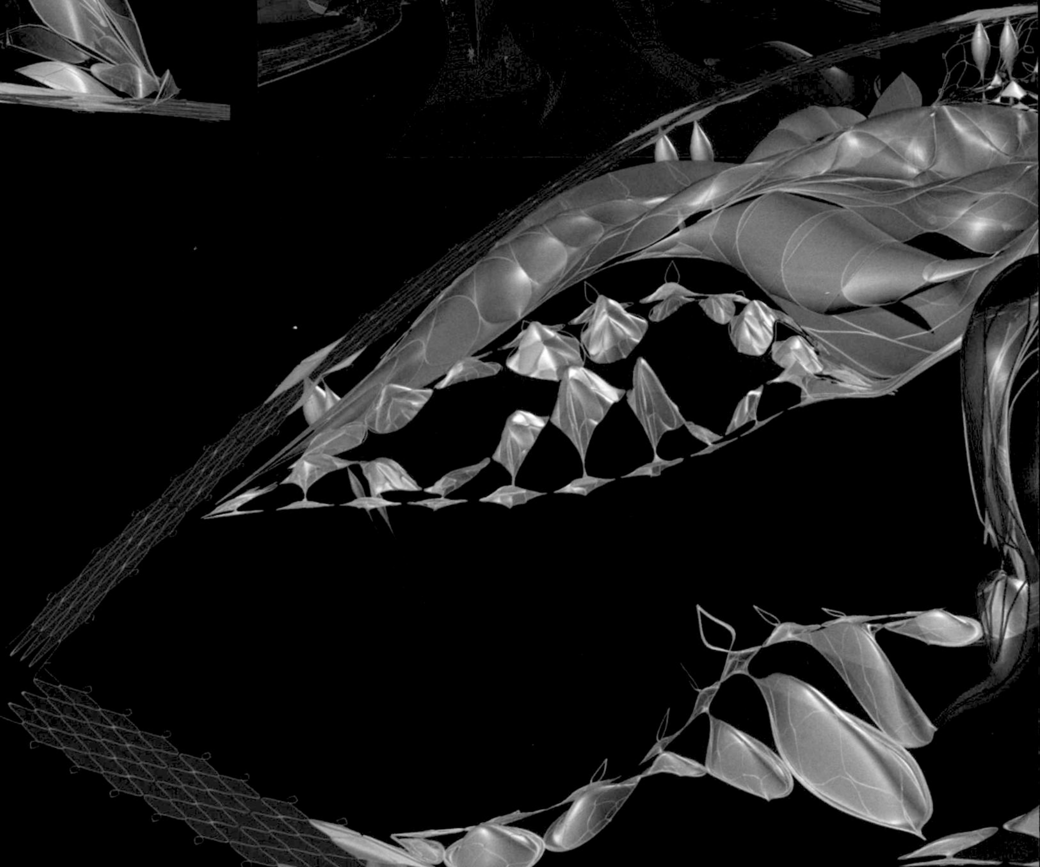

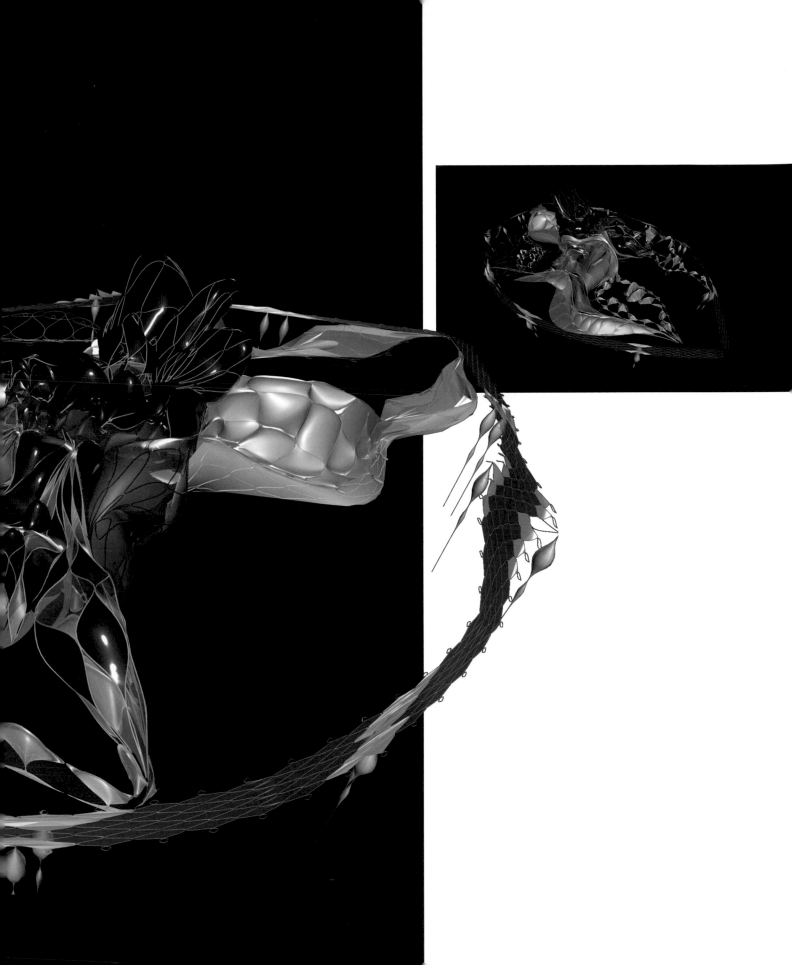

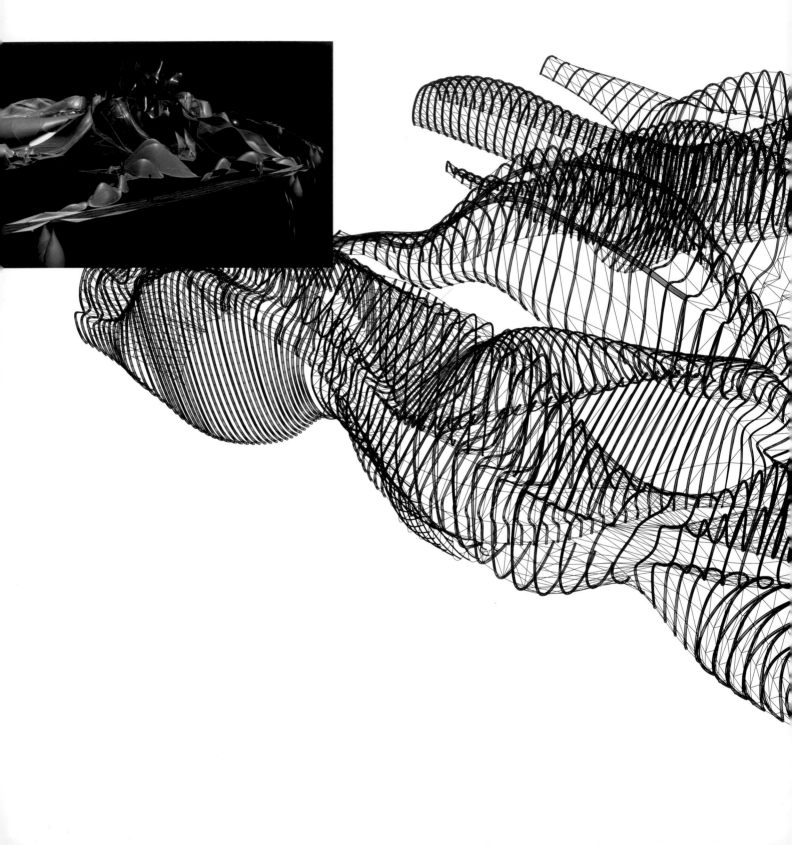

From left: Busan Concert Hall, perspective view; San Jose State University Museum of Art and Design, wire diagram and interior perspective

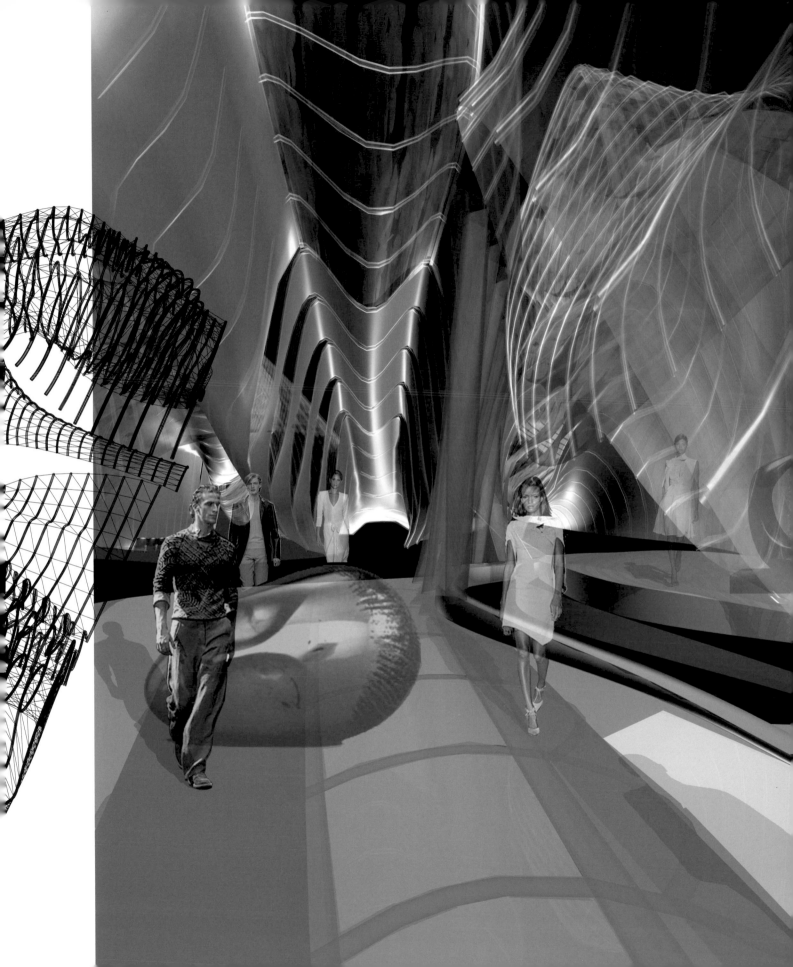

# SAN JOSE STATE UNIVERSITY MUSEUM OF ART AND DESIGN

## 2003 / San Jose, California

This project proposes a new museum for the university's school of art and design. In defining the facility's program, Xefirotarch took its cues from recent developments in contemporary art. The design is intended to embody the notion of art-as-experience rather than art-as-object; the building is conceived not as a static landmark, but instead as a dynamic conduit for the interaction of people and art.

The studio achieved this by generating the design primarily from circulation patterns. The first level serves as an interface between the museum and the campus environment; it engages and redirects existing pedestrian itineraries, facilitating the flow of visitors through the building and into the galleries. The second level houses classrooms, offices, and additional exhibition spaces. The natural circulation patterns of the building's interior allow for the movement of art objects as well as the activities of students and staff. These trajectories overlap with varying density, producing the three-dimensional lobes that form the interior volumes of the building.

The same spatial logic, based on a system of interdependent architectural programs, informs Xefirotarch's Landmark Tower / U2 Studio project of 2002. The tower's massive glass exterior houses an equally complex configuration of intersecting public and private spaces, and its animalistic form serves as a metaphor for the churning circulation patterns within the body of the building. Like that of the Landmark Tower, the exterior of the San Jose museum is generated by computer, but the evocative qualities of this design are very different. The swelling forms of the roofline, which is built up through overlapping layers rather than appearing as a single contoured surface, are meant to reference dunes of shifting sand. Although interactions between visitors, students, staff, and art may be in constant flux, the building's form literally and metaphorically roots the museum in the surrounding campus.

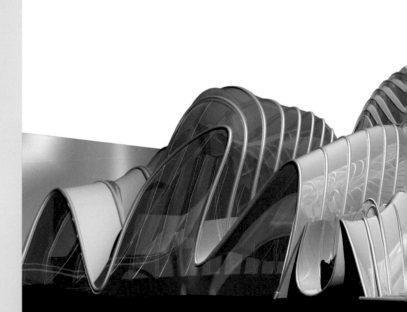

Clockwise from top left: San Jose State University Museum of Art and Design, conceptual site rendering, first-floor plan, and exterior perspective

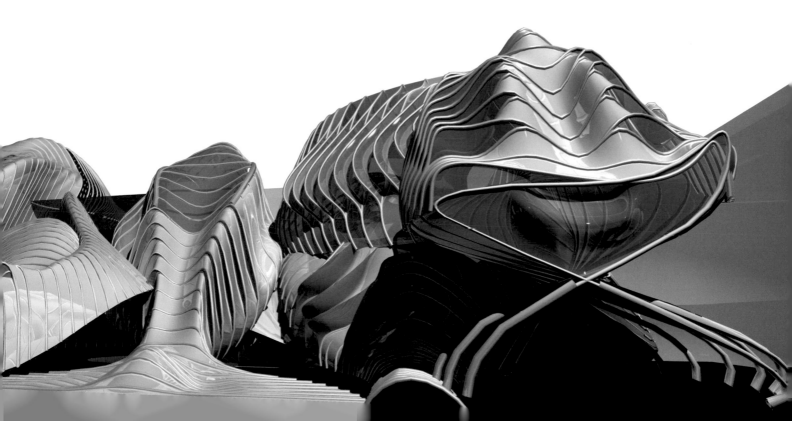

## SUR

### 2005 / Long Island City, New York

Xefirotarch's winning entry in the MoMA/P.S.1 Young Architects Program was installed in P.S.1's courtyard and served as the venue for its summer music series. Beneath a canopy of leaflike, concrete-colored forms made from fabric sheathing and aluminum tubes, visitors lounged on eccentrically shaped fiberglass benches and platforms coated in slick race-car red. The title, taken from a popular Argentinean tango, references the rhythmic forms of the architecture as well as the festival atmosphere. Grotesque yet playful, the pavilion was among Xefirotarch's first built designs in the United States.

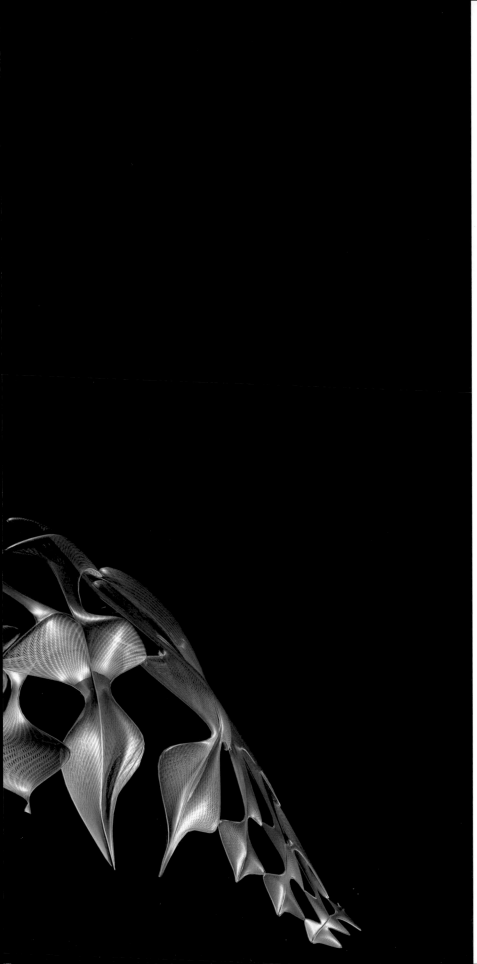

From left: *Sur*, oblique perspectives, installation view, and detail of canopy structure

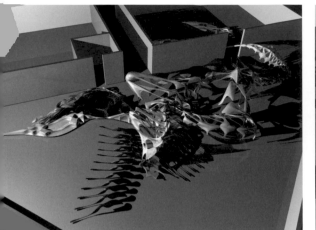

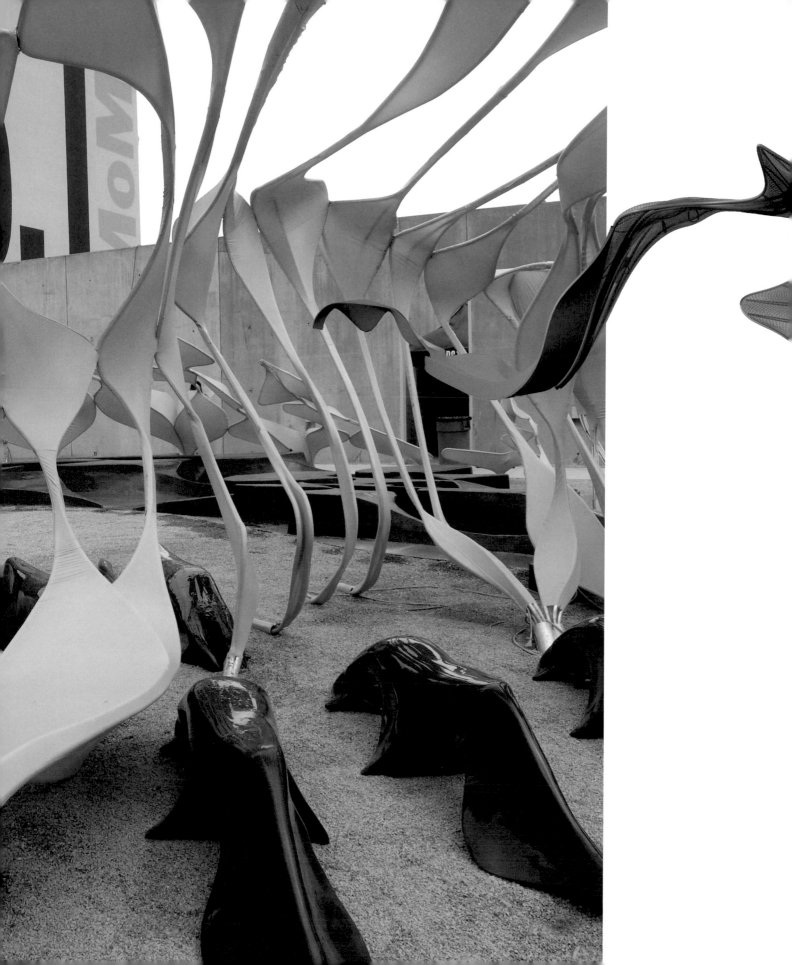

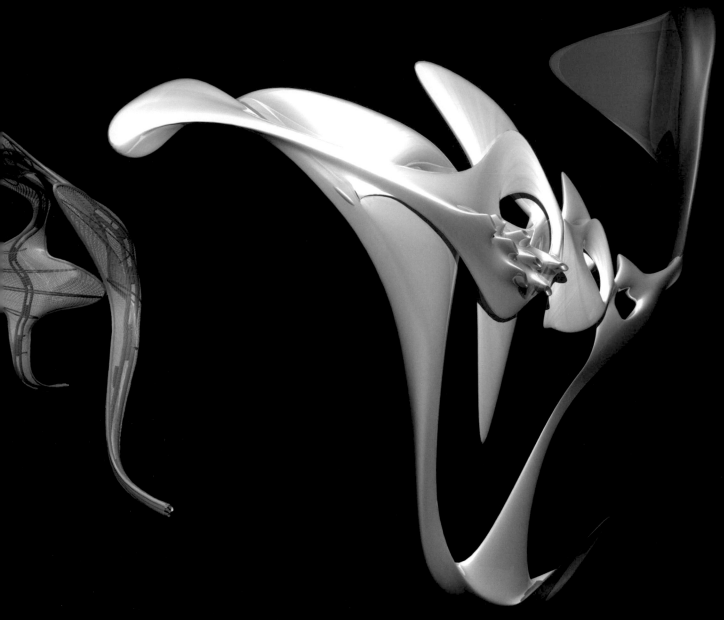

## CELL CONCEPT: EARPHONE AND DISPLAY SYSTEM
### 2005–6

In 2005 Xefirotarch began designing an earphone and a related retail storage and display system. The cell phone accessory, a flexible silicone membrane that the studio describes as a "technological prosthetic," sprouts from the ear, wraps around the jawline like a tattoo, and tapers to a small viewing screen in front of the eye. When not in use, it folds into the cell phone and the entire unit is enveloped, like an embryo, in a translucent polyurethane pouch. The store-display design extends this purely biological aesthetic: A network of wired, programmable cells attaches together with Velcro-like bristles. Like DNA, the cells function both individually (as shelves and recharging units) and collectively (as a system of walls and structures that may be customized to fit the specific needs of each space).

From left: *Sur*, detail of canopy structure; Cell Concept, renderings of earphone and storage pouch

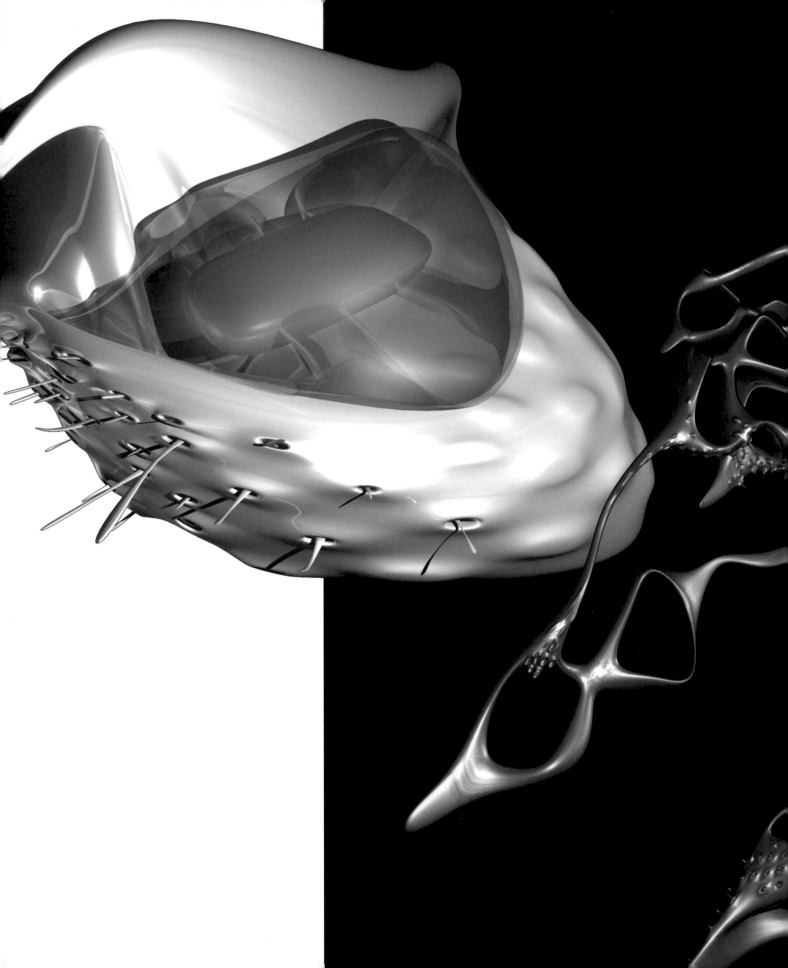

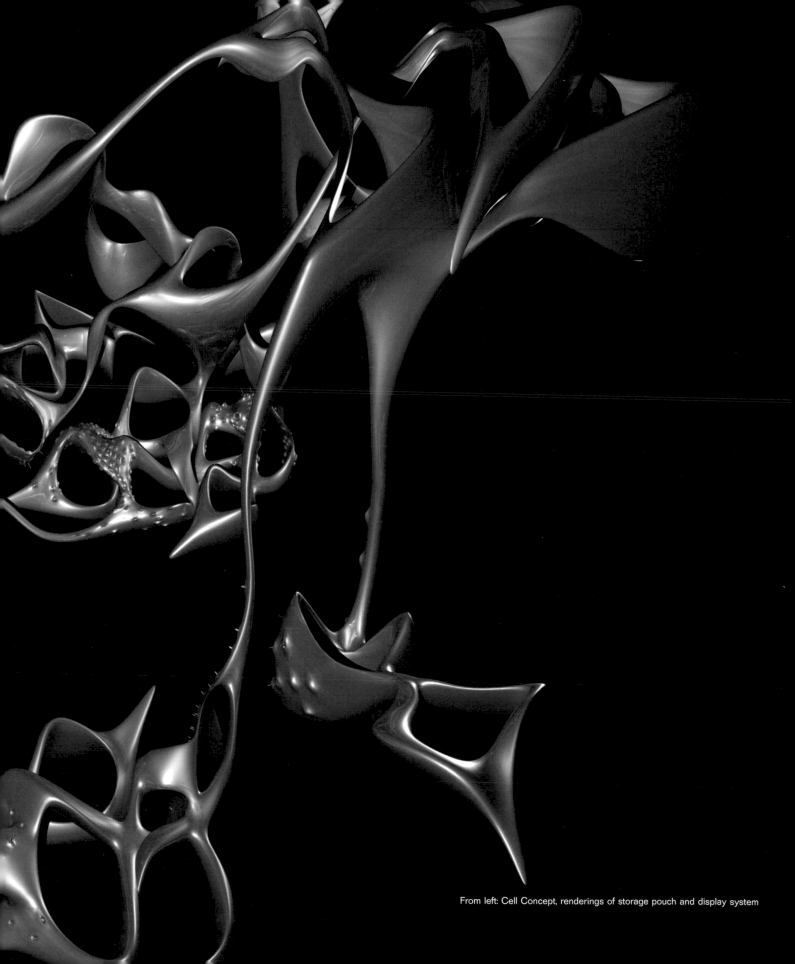

From left: Cell Concept, renderings of storage pouch and display system

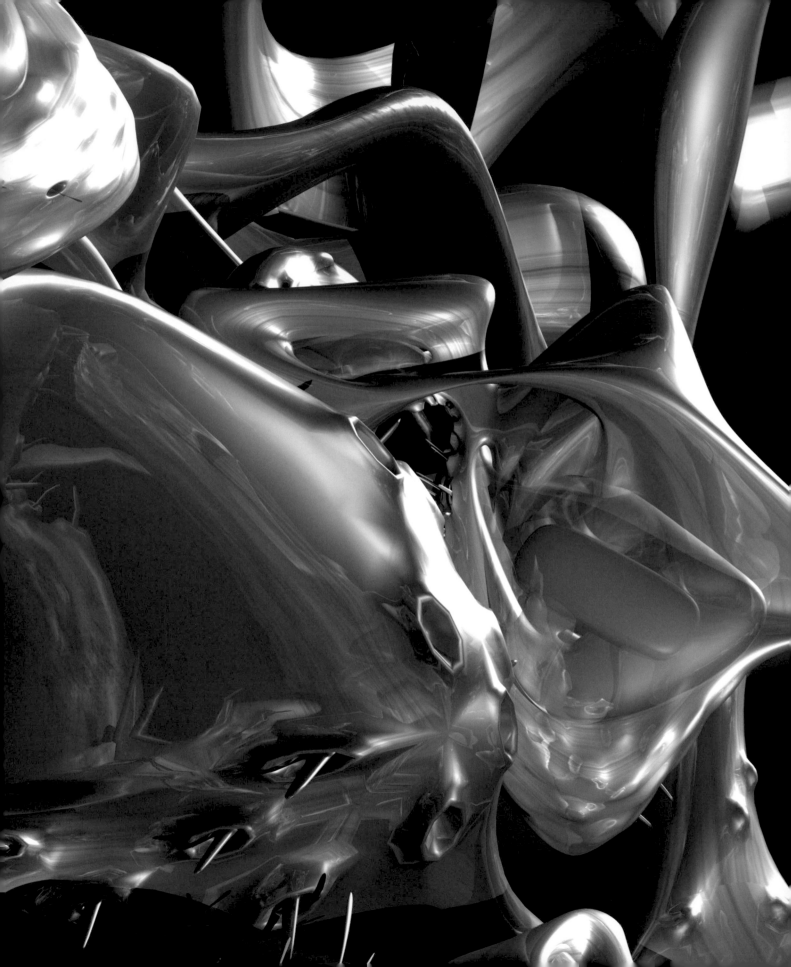

Cell Concept, rendering of display system

# DIRECTOR'S STATEMENT

**Neal Benezra**

Welcome to the fourth installment of SFMOMA's Design Series, dedicated to the exhibition and publication of innovative developments in contemporary design. Since its inception in 2003, the series has investigated work by the Manhattan architecture studio ROY, the San Francisco industrial design firm fuseproject, and the New York graphic designers 2x4. With *Xefirotarch* we return to architecture, examining the futuristic forms of Los Angeles–based Hernán Díaz Alonso. Rendered using the tools of digital design, Xefirotarch's projects—from master plans to museum buildings to watches and other objects—may appear to have little connection to the conventions of architecture as we know it. Yet, as curator Joseph Rosa explains in his catalogue essay. Díaz Alonso's biomorphic designs are both buildable and theoretically grounded, drawing on the language of cinema as well as those of painting, sculpture, and other art disciplines. Díaz Alonso views his projects as interlinked families, with elements mutating fluidly from building to building, installation to object; with his predilection for grotesque, often animal-like forms, he may be credited with reintroducing an experimental notion of figuration into contemporary architectural practice. We are delighted to present his first solo museum exhibition, which bears the additional distinction of being the first Design Series presentation to tour internationally.

This project was conceived by Joseph Rosa, SFMOMA's former curator of architecture and design, who established the Design Series and saw through this exhibition after assuming his new role as John H. Bryan Curator of Architecture and Design at the Art Institute of Chicago. We are grateful to Joe for his skillful leadership of the Museum's design program and for his ongoing dedication to the series. In the wake of his departure, Ruth Keffer, acting department head, has ably guided this project to fruition and deserves warm thanks for her skillful coordination and goodwill.

The curators join me in thanking SFMOMA's trustees, the architecture and design accessions committee, and A+D Forum for their ongoing advocacy of the Museum's design programming. This presentation is sponsored by Christine and Michael Murray, Nancy and Steven H. Oliver, the LEF Foundation, and an anonymous donor, to whom we extend gratitude for their generous support. We also thank the FRAC Centre, Orléans, France, for loaning work to the exhibition, and our tour venues—MAK, the Austrian Museum of Applied Arts / Contemporary Art, Vienna; the Architectural Association, London; and the Art Institute of Chicago—for their commitment to Xefirotarch's work.

For their many contributions to the project, I would like to acknowledge the following SFMOMA staff members: Michelle Barger, conservator; Ruth Berson, deputy director, exhibitions and collections; Olga Charyshyn, registrar; Alexander Cheves, senior museum preparator; Chad Coerver, director of publications; Steve Dye, exhibitions technical manager; Elizabeth Epley. assistant director of development, donor services; Jonathan Lehman, development assistant; Karen Levine, managing editor, publications; Andrea Morgan, associate director of development, foundation and government support; Apollonia Morrill, managing editor, communications; Terril Neely, senior designer; Kent Roberts, exhibitions design manager and chief preparator; Greg Sandoval, manager, adult interpretive programs; Jillian Slane, administrative assistant, exhibitions; Jennifer Sonderby, head of graphic design; Lindsey Westbrook, publications coordinator; Robyn Wise, public relations associate; and Jessica Woznak, exhibitions coordinator. Thanks are also due to curatorial associate Darrin Alfred and administrative assistant Eve Wickman for their support of all Architecture and Design Department activities.

Finally, this exhibition and catalogue would not have been possible without the close collaboration of Hernán Díaz Alonso and his associates at Xefirotarch, particularly Hunter Knight, Robert Mezquiti, Mirai Morita, Drura Parrish, Josh Taron, Ben Toam, and Jeremy Stoddart.

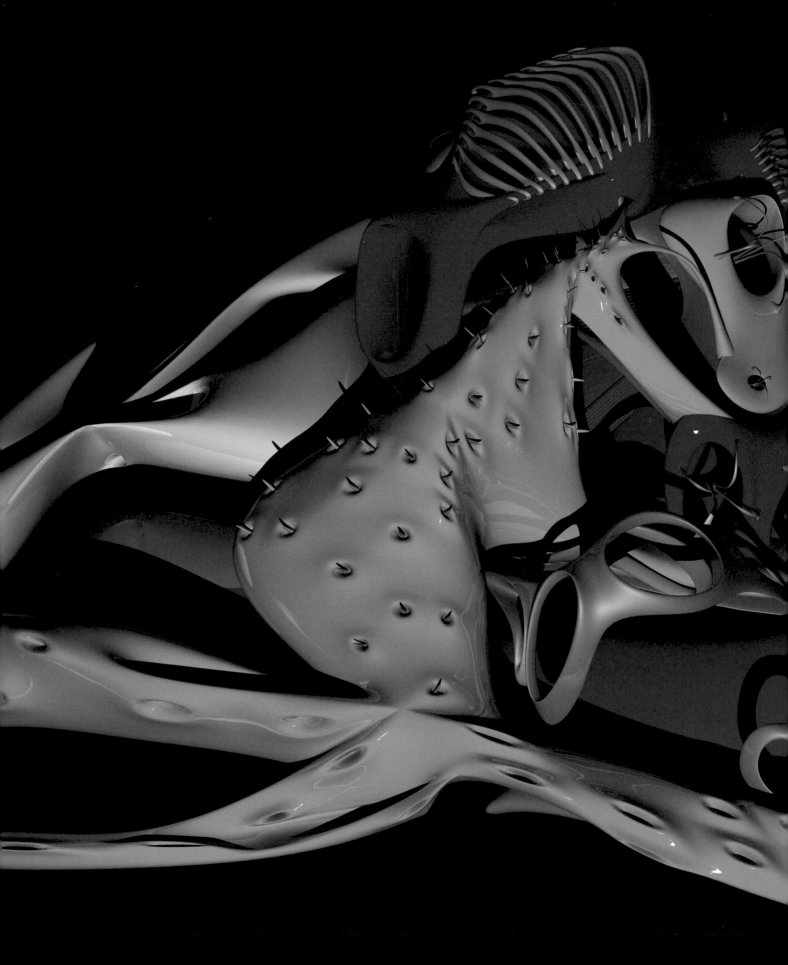

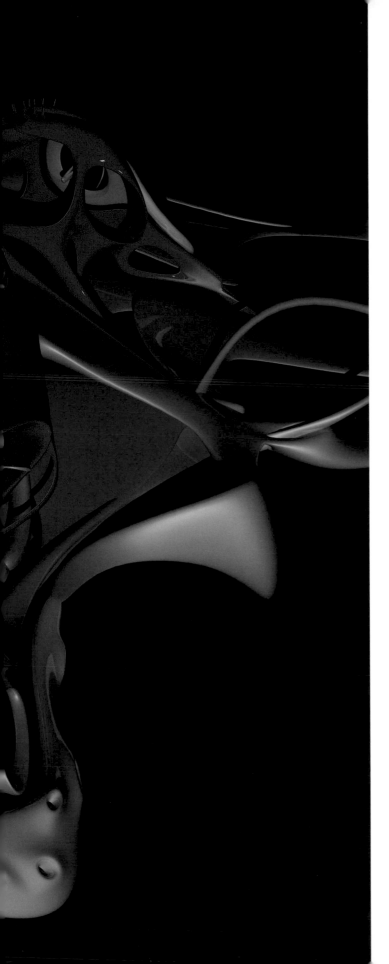

# MONSTROUS TRAITS: THE ARCHITECTURE OF XEFIROTARCH

Joseph Rosa

During the years of the War from 1914 to 1918, and for several years thereafter . . . young architects . . . seem to have been unusually active intellectually. The most important architectural innovations of the previous twenty or thirty years could now be correlated and, as it were, digested. . . . Many young architects also developed close personal associations with painters and sculptors of their own generation, often coming to accept rather completely their increasingly rigid abstract doctrines as a new gospel for all the arts. At the fringes of advanced experimentation architecture, painting and sculpture came very close [together]. . . . Indeed, in a certain theoretical sense, the three arts really merged in the[ir] constructions.
—Henry-Russell Hitchcock, *Painting Toward Architecture*[1]

The above passage looks back on the early-twentieth-century architectural innovations canonized in *Modern Architecture— International Exhibition*, the landmark 1932 presentation organized by Hitchcock and Philip Johnson for the Museum of Modern Art in New York, but it could just as easily describe the practice of avant-garde architecture today. Since its inception in the early 1990s, digital architecture has expanded into widening frontiers, fusing with other disciplines and theory to enable unexpected formal explorations, embody diverse ideologies, and generate new typologies

Emotional Rescue, installation view
2002 / Los Angeles

Queens Museum of Art, wire diagram of proposed extension
2002 / New York

that are changing the way architecture is fabricated, aestheticized, and understood.[2] As the discipline has matured, Hernán Díaz Alonso, the principal of Xefirotarch, has emerged as a significant figure; his studio's grotesquely hybrid, animal-like forms exemplify just how far digital practice has come in the past decade.

Born in Buenos Aires in 1969, Díaz Alonso received his bachelor's degree in architecture in 1995 from the College of Architecture, Planning, and Design at the National University of Rosario, Argentina. He then went on to earn a master's in advanced architectural design at Columbia University's Graduate School of Architecture, Planning, and Preservation, graduating with honors in 1999. Yet Díaz Alonso had already succeeded in launching his career prior to relocating to New York to attend Columbia. From 1995 to 1998 he ran a small studio in Rosario, undertaking a variety of commissions—including retail spaces and a school renovation—in his home country. In 1996 he moved to Barcelona to work for Enric Miralles (1955–2000), a Spanish architect known for breaking down tactile forms into poetic components that appear almost cinematic in assembly.[3] After graduating from Columbia, Díaz Alonso spent a year in San Francisco working at Quezada Architecture, and then moved back to New York to become a senior designer for Peter D. Eisenman. In 2001 he established Xefirotarch and returned to the West Coast, this time to Los Angeles, to join the faculty of the Southern California Institute of Architecture (SCI-Arc). He is now a professor and thesis coordinator for the school's

graduate program, and since 2004 he has also served as an adjunct assistant professor at Columbia.

Díaz Alonso's graduate studies, coinciding as they did with the emergence of a new digital pedagogy in design, aligned him with a school of thought that was changing the very practice of architecture at that time. The early 1990s produced Columbia's first generation of digitally informed academics and practitioners, and by the late 1990s Bernard Tschumi, then dean of the Graduate School of Architecture, Planning, and Preservation, had enlisted leading proponents of this thinking—Stanley Allen, Jeffrey Kipnis, Greg Lynn, William MacDonald, Hani Rashid, and Jesse Reiser—as adjunct faculty. The latter half of the decade saw the emergence of a second wave of digitally literate studios—including servo, PATTERNS / Marcelo Spina, and Xefirotarch—led by designers whose methodologies were more theoretically grounded, demonstrating a willingness to fold narratives and techniques from other disciplines into an architectural framework. As digital practice has matured, younger designers are again looking toward avant-garde figures of earlier generations, particularly those of the post-1968 era who drew on the discourses of Conceptual art, linguistics, semiotics, film theory, and the mass media to generate new forms of architecture.[4]

Díaz Alonso's debt to his training at Columbia is reflected in his design process, which revolves around formal genealogies and results in what he calls families of design:

Projects are the carriers of ideas[;] they move, mutate, duplicate them in order to produce a genealogy that will go from former to future generations of projects. Therefore, the modus operandi is set up by families of design. Unlike arborous genealogical organizations, the structures of these families [have] no hierarchical organization[;] they branch out and expand in different directions. The initial idea of a project could come from a small part of a previous one. Consequently mobility is always present in the designs, as a mechanism to produce constant change.[5]

Xefirotarch's proposals thus share certain genealogical characteristics, producing an architectural vocabulary unique to Díaz Alonso's work. The studio tends to heighten characteristics from one project to the next; like genetic mutations, traits evolve in form and substance as they pass from design to design. Viewed together, the ensuing groupings become family portraits of sorts. The winning competition entry for Lexington Metropolitan Plaza (2001–4), for instance, was one of the first projects to gain recognition for Xefirotarch. Its genealogy can be mapped through *Emotional Rescue*, a 2002 installation for the SCI-Arc Gallery in Los Angeles, as well as a 2002 proposal for the expansion of the Queens Museum of Art in New York. When asked to exhibit the Lexington Plaza design at the Venice Biennale's 2004 architecture exhibition, Xefirotarch integrated elements of *Emotional Rescue*—transparent enclosures

containing flowers that decayed over the course of the installation—into the earlier project's landscape, rendering it both the forebear and the progeny of its own formal genealogy.

Xefirotarch exploits this methodology without regard for scale; an element of a building can be repurposed as a vase, while a plate can become a city's master plan. For a 2002 project known as Mutant Manners, a single deformed matrix generated a complete line of plates, glasses, and napkin holders; a vase; and a cell phone. An offshoot of the Queens Museum proposal, Mutant Manners eventually evolved into the concept for the 2002 Bondis Bus Shelters. Another grouping that illustrates this type of migration begins with *Be-Boop* (2002), a proposed installation in San José, Costa Rica. The design, which was never executed, centers on an interior atrium space that is occupied and overcome by a looming cellular form. Replicated and joined with other elements, the same modulated form reappears in larger scale in Xefirotarch's 2003 proposal for a master plan, a concert hall, and ancillary accommodations in the port area of Busan, South Korea. In 2004 the studio revised the Busan master plan for the 2004 *Archilab* exhibition in Orléans, France, and also expanded the concert hall component for the Venice Biennale. These refinements, in turn, became central to *Sur*, a 2005 installation for the Museum of Modern Art / P.S.1 Young Architects Program in Long Island City, New York. Fluid and self-referential, Xefirotarch's genealogical approach recently spawned an entirely new family of design based on the Cell Concept (2005–6). Here, cellular units proliferate from mobile phones to retail interiors,

Mutant Manners, rendering of preliminary matrix
2002

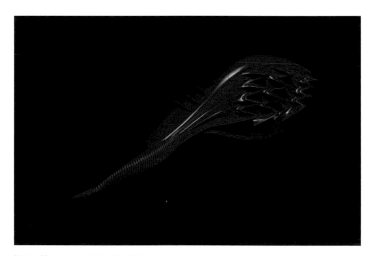

Mutant Manners, rendering of cell phone

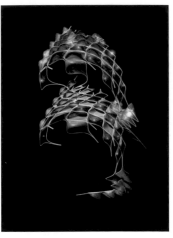

**Be-Boop, structural rendering**
2002 / San José, Costa Rica

**Be-Boop, detail of model**

with each mutation augmenting the cells' formal characteristics. The studio has continued this line of inquiry with the Art Hotel (2005–), a high-rise proposal for the province of Puerto Plata in the Dominican Republic.

Xefirotarch's genealogies emerge from an evolutionary trajectory, beginning with abstract formal elements that are then altered or combined to create hybrid structures. Characterized by Díaz Alonso as "singular surfaces,"[6] the projects that belong to the Lexington Plaza family—with the exception of the 2002 Landmark Tower / U2 Studio—are generally nonfigurative in conception and geometry. (Sphinxlike in character, the Landmark Tower is a transitional project that also has ties to *Be-Boop*.) The designs in the *Be-Boop* family represent a move toward animal-like forms, but their "legs," "tentacles," and other figurative elements rarely coalesce into a complete, anthropomorphic body. Supple, curvaceous, and ambiguous, most of the projects in this family feature surfaces with repetitive patterning. The fleshy, uneven forms of the Cell Concept, on the other hand, are riddled with irregular protrusions that sprout wildly from follicular depressions.

As Xefirotarch's genealogies evolve, they tend to become more monstrous in construction. Greg Lynn, the leading figure in the birth of digital architecture (and, like Díaz Alonso, a former protégé of Eisenman), has been a significant influence upon— and friend to—Xefirotarch's principal. Lynn's prolific early writings address the negation of the body as form: "Monstrosities are

bodies which seem to 'deviate from nature.' Bodies produced through combinatorial differentiation are not divisible by any single module; they are both irreducible unities and collections of heterogeneous elements; they are simultaneously a unified whole and freely associated parts."[7] Monstrous forms and their representations have often been intertwined with contemporary notions of beauty. As Umberto Eco points out in *History of Beauty*:

> Every culture has always accompanied its own concept of Beauty with its own idea of Ugliness. . . . [T]o Western eyes, certain fetishes and certain masks from other cultures seem to represent horrible or deformed creatures, while for natives they can be or could have been portrayals of positive values.
>
> Greek mythology possesses a wealth of creatures like fauns, Cyclopes, chimera, and minotaurs, or divinities like Priapus, considered monstrous and extraneous to the canons of Beauty . . . ; nonetheless, the attitude toward these entities was not always one of repugnance.[8]

Thus, depending on cultural context, the response to monstrosity can fluctuate between distaste and fascination, rendering anomaly both grotesque and sublime.

In architecture, beauty has been linked historically to the ideas of proportion and Cartesian form. Once architects venture into the realm of non-Cartesian form, normative notions of scale and beauty cease to apply. The sublime grotesque is thus crucial to the interpretation and codification of non-Cartesian forms. For Xefirotarch, the subversion of scale as a generative device for architecture is closely tied to a propensity for monstrous, hybrid constructions. While there are various ideologies behind the notion of the sublime, Immanuel Kant's 1790 *Critique of Judgement* is the most succinct when it comes to spatial characteristics. Kant defines two types of sublime, the mathematical and the dynamic. Of the former he writes:

> The feeling of the sublime is a pleasure . . . and involving emotional excitement it does not appear as the play, but

as the serious exercise, of the imagination. Accordingly, it cannot be united with sensuous charm; and as the mind is alternately attracted and repelled by the object, the satisfaction in the sublime implies not so much a positive pleasure as wonder or reverential awe, and may be called a negative pleasure.

The dynamic sublime, on the other hand, is described as follows:

Bold, overhanging and as it were threatening cliffs, masses of cloud piled up in the heavens and alive with lightning and peals of thunder, hurricanes bearing destruction in their path; these by their tremendous force dwarf our power of resistance into insignificance. But we are all the more attracted by their aspect the more fearful they are, when we are in a state of security; and we at once pronounce them sublime.[9]

Both definitions are useful for understanding Xefirotarch's architecture. The mathematical sublime addresses the transpositional notion of beauty as a negative pleasure, while the dynamic sublime is connected to the vastness of nature and its potential for devastation. Both, however, require a distancing device that allows the pleasures of the sublime to exist. In Xefirotarch's work, the conceptual overlay of cinematic logic becomes that device, allowing both forms of the sublime to operate simultaneously.

Díaz Alonso freely admits that he originally wanted to enroll in film school; however, his university had not yet instituted a film program, so he went into architecture instead. Throughout his career his designs have reflected a love of cinema. Xefirotarch's renderings frame design elements in storyboard fashion, drawing heavily on the conventions of science-fiction films. Cinematic logic also resonates throughout his families of design, whose fluid mutations of form unfold much like films are made: Just as movie scenes are rarely shot in sequence, design elements from later Xefirotarch projects often come back to inform their progenitors. Díaz Alonso, as he puts it, "assimilates architectural strategies with film" and operates aesthetically in "terms of images and cinematic effects."[10] His work,

as he describes it, is not about process but rather the exploration of technique:

Identity is no longer identified with notions of uniqueness but rather with those of alertness, alertness as a search for smooth renovation through a process of transformation as well as constant incorporation of information. The spatial effects of such design series are those of affected dense atmosphere that does not appeal to any pre-established imagery, but rather will insist on exploring innovative spatial qualities.[11]

The studio fosters the cinematic character of its digital drawings by employing stark black backgrounds; floating in this featureless atmosphere, the isolated forms resemble aliens or underwater sea creatures. Similarly, digitally milled models seem to mimic delicate internal organs or jellyfish. Even the spatial characteristics of Díaz Alonso's installations are informed by cinematic logic. The site contextualization of *Emotional Rescue* and *Sur* demonstrates that he knows how to manipulate space to create environments that are both compelling and disturbing. This particular skill, which may be attributed to his years working with Miralles and Eisenman as well as to his studies at Columbia, confirms that Xefirotarch's work is both theoretically grounded and eminently buildable.

Aside from their cinematic qualities, Xefirotarch's projects also draw on other forms of visual art, in particular the sculpture,

Busan Concert Hall, model
2003–4 / Busan, South Korea

Sangre, preliminary structural rendering
2006 / San Francisco

video, and film work of contemporary artist Matthew Barney (born 1967) and the paintings of Francis Bacon (1909–1992). Over the course of his five-part *CREMASTER* series (1994–2002), Barney deploys a wide array of characters, including a number of hybrid creatures, in highly choreographed cinematic narratives; he displays stills from the epic project in specially designed, "self-lubricating" white frames.[12] Like Barney, Díaz Alonso is extremely concerned with the ways in which his projects are framed and displayed. He controls their presentation by manipulating the background tonalities of his renderings and by consistently choosing red and silver surfaces for buildings and objects. A prime example is *Sangre* (2006): This installation, commissioned to house models for the San Francisco Museum of Modern Art's exhibition, is coated with patented, factory-issue Ferrari Red paint. In giving the project a title that means "blood" in Spanish (for Díaz Alonso, the form "manifests a state of coagulation"[13]), he betrays his interest in augmenting the emotional impact of his projects through textual reference. Similarly, several other Xefirotarch designs are named after songs by the Rolling Stones.

Bacon's paintings (and writings on Bacon's work) have influenced Díaz Alonso in very different, though no less significant, ways. Bacon's monstrous figures provide a key to understanding the indeterminate character of much of Xefirotarch's architecture. *Francis Bacon: The Logic of Sensation* by critic Gilles Deleuze is a touchstone of sorts for the architect. In it, Deleuze describes Bacon's approach to deformation and his ideological intentions:

> The deformations the body undergoes are also the *animal traits* of the head. This has nothing to do with a correspondence between animal forms and facial forms. The marks or traits of animality are not animal forms but rather the spirits that haunt the wiped-off parts, that pull at the head, individualizing and qualifying the head without a face. Bacon's technique of local scrubbing and asignifying traits take on a particular meaning here. Sometimes the human head is replaced by an animal, but it is not the animal as a form but rather the animal as a *trait*.[14]

Likewise, Díaz Alonso is not creating monsters; instead, he aims to identify traits or characteristics that might define—or obscure—his designs' organic forms.

It is this figurative aspect that differentiates Xefirotarch's hybrid practice from the rigorous abstraction of the predecessors discussed by Hitchcock in the epigraph to this essay. Like the architects of Hitchcock's generation, Xefirotarch draws freely from a wide range of visual-arts disciplines, but he combines these influences with digital manipulation and distortion to explore the limits of beauty and scale. Tracing formal mutations through genealogical family portraits, Díaz Alonso's monstrous constructions hover tantalizingly between the grotesque and the sublime, reintroducing an experimental notion of figuration to the pedagogy and practice of digital architecture.

## NOTES

This essay is based on seminar interviews with Hernán Díaz Alonso that took place at SCI-Arc on March 3, 2004, and March 24, 2005, augmented by private conversations between the author and the architect between spring 2005 and winter 2006.

1.  Henry-Russell Hitchcock, *Painting Toward Architecture* (New York: Duell, Sloan, and Pearce, 1948), 23.

2.  For more on digital architecture and its origins, see Joseph Rosa, *Next Generation Architecture: Folds, Blobs, and Boxes* (New York: Rizzoli, 2003), the revised version of a text that originally appeared in Joseph Rosa, *Folds, Blobs, and Boxes: Architecture in the Digital Era* (Pittsburgh: Heinz Architectural Center, Carnegie Museum of Art, 2001). See also Joseph Rosa, *ROY / design series 1* (San Francisco: San Francisco Museum of Modern Art, 2003); Frédéric Migayrou, *Non-Standard Architecture* (Paris: Centre Pompidou, 2004); Frédéric Migayrou and Marie-Ange Brayer, eds., *Archilab: Radical Experiments in Global Architecture* (London: Thames and Hudson, 2001); Branko Kolarevic, ed., *Architecture in the Digital Age: Design and Manufacturing* (New York: Spon Press, 2003); Branko Kolarevic and Ali M. Malkawi, eds., *Performative Architecture: Beyond Instrumentality* (New York: Spon Press, 2005); "Contemporary Processes in Architecture," ed. Ali Rahim, *Architectural Design* 70, no. 3 (June 2000); and *Metamorph: 9th International Architecture Exhibition* (New York: Rizzoli; Venice: Fondazione La Biennale di Venezia, 2004).

3.  Miralles's influence is easily recognizable in Díaz Alonso's recent digital work, particularly in installations such as *Emotional Rescue* (2002) and *Sur* (2005).

4.  For more on post-1968 avant-garde thinking, see Michael K. Hays, ed., *Architecture Theory Since 1968* (Cambridge, MA: MIT Press; New York: Columbia Books of Architecture, 1998).

5.  Jeffrey Kipnis, "Hernán Díaz Alonso, Xefirotarch," in *Sessions*, ed. Julianna Morais (Los Angeles: Southern California Institute of Architecture Press, 2004), unpaginated.

6.  Hernán Díaz Alonso, interview by the author, January 15, 2006.

7.  Greg Lynn, "Body Matters" (1995), in *Folds, Bodies, and Blobs: Collected Essays* (Brussels: La Lettre Volée, 1998), 141–42. For other writings by Lynn, see *Animate Form* (New York: Princeton Architectural Press, 1999).

8.  Umberto Eco, *History of Beauty*, trans. Alastair McEwen (New York: Rizzoli, 2004), 131, 133.

9.  Immanuel Kant, *The Critique of Judgement*, trans. J. C. Meredith (London: Oxford University Press, 1952), 490–91, 498–99.

10. Kipnis, "Hernán Díaz Alonso, Xefirotarch," unpaginated.

11. Ibid.

12. For more on Barney and the *CREMASTER* cycle, see Nancy Spector, *Matthew Barney: The CREMASTER Cycle* (New York: Solomon R. Guggenheim Foundation, 2003).

13. Díaz Alonso, interview by the author, January 15, 2006.

14. Gilles Deleuze, *Francis Bacon: The Logic of Sensation*, trans. Daniel W. Smith (Minneapolis: University of Minnesota Press, 2003), 19–20.

## LEXINGTON METROPOLITAN PLAZA

**Location:** Lexington, Kentucky
**Design:** 2001–4
**Status:** competition entry
**Size:** eight-acre site
**Client:** City of Lexington
**Design team:** Hernán Díaz Alonso and Florencia Pita with Kara Block, Laura Fehlberg, Bryan Flaig, Mark Nagis, Drura Parrish, Timothy Rives Rash II, Tony Thrim, and Evan Tribus

## BONDIS BUS SHELTERS

**Location:** New York
**Design:** 2002
**Status:** competition entry
**Size:** fifteen shelters, each 270 square feet
**Client:** *Core77*
**Design team:** Hernán Díaz Alonso with Evan Geisler and James Lowder

## EMOTIONAL RESCUE

**Location:** Southern California Institute of Architecture, Los Angeles
**Design:** 2002
**Status:** temporary installation, September 20–October 27, 2002
**Size:** 1,400 square feet
**Materials:** copper tubing, plastic, and roses
**Client:** Southern California Institute of Architecture
**Design team:** Hernán Díaz Alonso with Debbie Chiu, Jennifer Dunlop, Evan Geisler, Asako Hiraoka, Randal Larsen, Makoto Mizutani, Timothy Rives Rash II, Kevin Sperry, Simon Story, Sandy Watts, and Jeremy Whitener

## LANDMARK TOWER / U2 STUDIO

**Location:** Dublin, Ireland
**Design:** 2002
**Status:** competition entry
**Size:** 85,000 square feet
**Client:** U2 and Dublin Dockland Development Authority
**Design team:** Hernán Díaz Alonso with Eric Cheong, Timothy Rives Rash II, and Tony Thrim

## SAN JOSE STATE UNIVERSITY MUSEUM OF ART AND DESIGN

**Location:** San Jose, California
**Design:** 2003
**Status:** competition entry
**Size:** 35,000 square feet
**Client:** San Jose State University School of Art and Design
**Design team:** Hernán Díaz Alonso with Eric Cheong, Timothy Rives Rash II, and Tony Thrim in partnership with Alfred Quezada Jr. and Mason Kirby (Quezada Architecture)

## BUSAN MASTER PLAN AND CONCERT HALL

**Location:** Busan, South Korea
**Design:** 2003–4
**Status:** competition entry
**Size:** 550-acre site (master plan); 350,000 square feet (concert hall)
**Client:** Busan Metropolitan City
**Design team:** Hernán Díaz Alonso with Laura Fehlberg, Bryan Flaig, Asako Hiraoka, Mark Nagis, Drura Parrish, Timothy Rives Rash II, Kevin Sperry, Richard "Doc" Bailey (image savant), Bruce Danziger (Arup LA), and Peter Zellner (Zellner / Design Planning Research)

## JUMPING JACK FLASH WATCH
**Design:** 2004—
**Status:** concept
**Client:** Timex and *Core77*
**Design team:** Hernán Díaz Alonso with Laura Fehlberg, Brian Flaig, Mark Nagis, and Drura Parrish

## ART HOTEL
**Location:** Puerto Plata Province, Dominican Republic
**Design:** 2005—
**Status:** concept
**Size:** seven-acre site (resort grounds); 130,000 square feet (hotel)
**Client:** Boykin Curry
**Design team:** Hernán Díaz Alonso with Hunter Knight, Robert Mezquiti, Mirai Morita, Jeremy Stoddart, Josh Taron, Ben Toam, and Drura Parrish (Spectrum 3D)

## SUR
**Location:** P.S.1 Contemporary Art Center, Long Island City, New York
**Design:** 2005
**Status:** temporary installation, June 26—September 3, 2005
**Size:** 5,000 square feet
**Materials:** aluminum tubing, Lycra, and fiberglass
**Client:** The Museum of Modern Art, New York, and P.S.1 Contemporary Art Center
**Design team:** Hernán Díaz Alonso with Chris Arntzen, Jee Hee Farris, Bryan Flaig, Hunter Knight, Mark Nagis, Nicholas Pisca, Casey Rhem, and Ben Toam
**Installation team:** Jeff Chen, Jayson Christopher, Casey Crawmer, Toru Hasgawa, Sunnie Joh, Chris Kanipe, Eric Lilhanand, Carolyn Matsumoto, Casey McSweeney, Robert Mezquiti, Mirai Morita, Lisa Schwert, and Dong-Ping Wong
**Additional assistance:** Gaby Anker, Chris Arntzen, Chris Chen, Montana Cherney, Ben Cohen, Blake Dane, Serena Davis, Brock Desmit, Lili Dirks-Goodman, Paul Duston-Munoz, David Fano, Steve Fuchs, Owen Gherst, Dina Giordano, Roberto Goyeneche, Noriaki Hanaoka, June Hayatsu, Moira Henry, Dave Hood, Frauke Hormann, Greg Kay, Hunter Knight, Ben Kohen, Mo Chingying Lai, Lionel Lambourn, Amiee Lee, Aaron Leppanen, Elizabeth Marley, Katie Mearns, Santino Medina, Cristina Milleur, Naoko Miyano, Kirsten Moore, Jonathan Morefield, Jared Nash Olmsted, Ben Porto, Kevin Regaldo, Lauren Rosenbloom, Katrina Slupinski, Jeremy Stoddart, Josh Taron, Marina Topunova, Rain Wang, Alex Webb, Trent Welcome, Jonah Wortman, Arnold Wu, Li Xu, Paul Yoo, and Lauren Zuzack
**Executive architect:** Timothy Rives Rash II
**Associate architect:** Alexis Rochas
**Fabrication:** Gary Abraham, Scott Abraham, and Drura Parrish (Spectrum 3D)
**Engineering:** Bruce Danzinger (Arup LA)

## CELL CONCEPT: EARPHONE AND DISPLAY SYSTEM
**Design:** 2005—6
**Status:** concept
**Materials:** carbon fiber, aluminum, silicone, and polyurethane
**Design team:** Hernán Díaz Alonso with Robert Mezquiti, Mirai Morita, Jeremy Stoddart, Josh Taron, and Ben Toam

## SANGRE
**Location:** San Francisco Museum of Modern Art (and tour venues for the exhibition *Xefirotarch*)
**Design:** 2006
**Status:** temporary installation, March 31—September 17, 2006 (exhibition touring through 2008)
**Size:** 250 square feet
**Materials:** Styrofoam, urethane coating, automobile paint, and hardware
**Client:** San Francisco Museum of Modern Art
**Design team:** Hernán Díaz Alonso with Hunter Knight, Robert Mezquiti, Mirai Morita, Jeremy Stoddart, Josh Taron, and Ben Toam
**Associate architect:** Drura Parrish

## SELECTED BIBLIOGRAPHY

Bernstein, Fred. "A Timely Lesson in the Life and Function of Forms." *Architectural Record* 193, no. 9 (September 2005): 73–74.

Boira, Francisco David, and Zoe Coombes. "Hernán Díaz Alonso: Winner of This Year's MoMA/P.S.1 Young Architects Program." *Archinect,* April 11, 2005. http://archinect.com/features/article.php?id=17584_0_23_0_C.

Chang, Jade. "Made in Hollywood." *Metropolis* 24, no. 11 (July 2005): 126–29, 158–59.

Di Cristina, Giuseppa. "Agora: Dreams and Visions." *L'Arca,* no. 191 (April 2004): 32–39.

Forster, Kurt W., ed. *Metamorph: 9th International Architecture Exhibition.* New York: Rizzoli; Venice: Fondazione La Biennale di Venezia, 2004.

Hagberg, Eva. "Urban Journal: Hernán Díaz Alonso's Critical Architecture." *Metropolis,* June 13, 2005. http://www. metropolismag.com/cda/story.php?artid=1437.

Holt, Steven Skov, and Mara Holt Skov. *Blobjects and Beyond: The New Fluidity in Design.* San Francisco: Chronicle Books, 2005.

Horauf, Simon. "*Sur*—From the Beauty to the Beast." *(inside),* no. 38 (2005): 80–83.

Kipnis, Jeffrey. "Hernán Díaz Alonso, Xefirotarch." In *Sessions,* edited by Julianna Morais. Los Angeles: Southern California Institute of Architecture Press, 2004.

Laster, Paul. "Interview." *Artkrush,* no. 11 (July 27, 2005). http://www.artkrush.com/mailer/issue11/#interview.

Lipton, Shana Ting. "The Living House: Architecture Gets Organic." *res* 6, no. 2 (March–April 2003): 68–70.

Lootsma, Bart, et al. *Archilab Orléans 2004: La ville à nu / The Naked City.* Orléans, France: Editions HYX, 2004.

Muschamp, Herbert. "Thinking Big: A Plan for Ground Zero and Beyond." *New York Times Magazine,* September 8, 2002. http://www.nytimes.com/library/magazine/home/20020908mag-index.html.

Ouroussoff, Nicolai. "At P.S.1, an Illusion of Tents Billowing in the Breeze." *New York Times,* July 14, 2005.

Rosa, Joseph, ed. *Glamour: Fashion, Industrial Design, Architecture.* San Francisco: San Francisco Museum of Modern Art; New Haven, CT: Yale University Press, 2004.

———. *Next Generation Architecture: Folds, Blobs, and Boxes.* New York: Rizzoli, 2003.

Ryan, Zoe. "Big *Sur* Makes Waves." *Blueprint,* no. 234 (September 2005): 28.

Speaks, Michael. "Design Intelligence, Part 8: Hernán Díaz Alonso." *A + U: Architecture and Urbanism,* no. 394 (July 2003): 140–47.

Tretiack, Philippe. "Salles de concert: Venise donne le ton." *Beaux Arts,* no. 246 (November 2004): 18.

Vogliazzo, Maurizio. "Archilab 2004." *L'Arca,* no. 197 (November 2004): 24–35.

Whitehead, Ingrid. "Hernán Díaz Alonso Seeks a Balance between Technology and Romanticism." *Architectural Record* 189, no. 12 (December 2001): 64–69.